To parents and carers

Lots of these activities will involve you, or others at home, child to do alone. Most take about 10 to 15 minutes.

Some are for practice and some are meant to get children to think – but they are all intended to be enjoyable. You don't have to teach any maths – just join in when your child needs a partner to work with.

Getting started

Make sure that your child understands what they are expected to do. Read through the activity with them, then encourage them to talk about how they are going to tackle it. This is usually enough to get them going.

Even if you are not directly involved in an activity, ask questions about it and make positive comments. If an answer is wrong, you can still say things like 'That's interesting. Let's check it together.'

Mental arithmetic and times-tables

Most of the activities involve mental arithmetic because this is even more important than written arithmetic. Your child should know by heart the sum or difference of pairs of numbers such as 7 + 9 or 15 – 8. Get them to practise adding or taking away two-digit numbers in their heads. Knowing pairs of numbers that make 100 is very helpful.

By now children should know all the times-tables by heart. In this book the focus is on the 6, 7, 8 and 9 times-tables, with revision of the tables that have been learned earlier. Ask questions at odd moments: 'What are six nines?' 'How many sevens in sixty-three?' 'Divide fifty-six by eight.' 'Tell me one fifth of forty-five.'

Help your child to see that when numbers are multiplied or divided by 10 or 100 the digits move one or two places to the left or right, and empty places are filled with zeros.

Making it enjoyable

Home maths is meant to be fun. Carry on with any of the activities as long as your child is keen. Adapt the ideas and vary the rules as much as you like. Time how long an exercise takes, then try it again after a month to see if it can be done more quickly.

Let your child see that you too enjoy the activities that you do together. If you say 'That was fun!' then your child is very likely to think the same.

Anita Straker

1

Ask an adult to time you.
You need pencil and paper. Write only the answers.

1. Two squared. *4*
2. 102 × 3. *306*
3. ⅒ of 150. *15*
4. 69 + 42. *111*
5. 3000 − 1997. *1003*
6. Roughly, what is 29 × 29 *900*
7. How many nines in 36? *4*
8. Write **62 248** in words. *sixty two thousand two hundred and forty eight*
9. 14 + ☐ = 93.
10. What is next: 21, 28, 35, … ?
11. Write ⁹⁄₁₀ as a decimal.
12. Find the product of 46 and 100.
13. How many millimetres is 4 metres?
14. Double 56.

2

Magic money

Do this on your own.
You need pencil and paper.

£2.80		£2.40
		£2.90

Each row, column and diagonal of this magic square adds up to £7.50.
Copy and complete it.

Draw a new square with 50p less in each box.
Is it still magic? What is the total of each line now? Check each one.

Add sums of money
Think logically

3 Birthday

Play this with a partner.

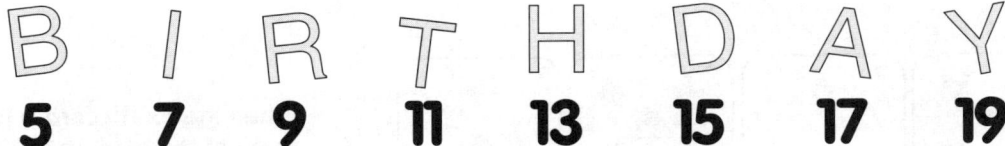

B I R T H D A Y
5 7 9 11 13 15 17 19

Each letter has a value.

Add up the numbers in the words below.

Your partner should check and say if you are right.

1	HAY	5	RAT	9	HAIR
2	RIB	6	ADD	10	TIDY
3	BAD	7	BIT	11	HARD
4	HID	8	DART	12	THAT

Think of more words using the letters of BIRTHDAY.

Ask your partner to work out what they are worth.

You must say if your partner is right.

Add several numbers less than 20

4 Eighteens

Two people can play.
You need a pack of playing cards.
Use the ace to 10 of each suit.

Shuffle the cards.
Place them face down in a pile.
Take turns to take a card.
Place it face up in front of you.

The first player to have three cards to total exactly 18 scores 3 points.
If your first three cards do not add up to 18, keep going until three of your whole set of cards total 18.

When the fourth card is taken, three of the cards total 18, because 8 + 7 + 3 = 18

Take turns to go first.
The winner is the first player to get 30 points.

Change the rules
a. Make a total 15 or 16 or 17.
b. Aim for five cards to total 25.

Add several small numbers
Use addition facts to 20

5

Ask an adult to read you these.
You need pencil and paper. Write only the answers.

1. Four squared.
2. Nine nines.
3. Add 13, 8 and 4.
4. Take 7 from 9 plus 8.
5. 35 divided by 7.
6. Double 78.
7. Four sixes.
8. How many days in 9 weeks?
9. One tenth of 1000.
10. Take £14.45 from £20.
11. How many 50p coins make £13.
12. Write 6 metres in millimetres.
13. Divide 160 by 4.
14. What is the product of 152 and 10?

6

You need pencil and paper. Write only the answers.

1. Sam is 9 years old. Does he weigh 40 kg or 400 g?
2. How many lengths of 6 cm can you cut from 50 cm of ribbon?
3. Which of these numbers is divisible by three: 26, 27, 28, 29?
4. CDs are £7 each. How much for a pack of 5?
5. What is the change from £1 for 2 comics at 34p each?
6. What is the total of three 50p and nine 5p coins?
7. Round 362 to the nearest hundred.
8. How many pairs can be made from 43 socks?
9. What number multiplied by itself gives 16?
10. What number is shown on this scale?

7 Target

Do this by yourself.

You need pencil and paper.

Use three numbers from this set each time.

Copy and complete these.

1. ... + ... + ... = **109**
2. ... + ... + ... = **78**
3. ... + ... + ... = **124**
4. ... + ... + ... = **87**
5. ... + ... + ... = **103**
6. ... + ... + ... = **102**

Add three two-digit numbers
Work out a strategy

8

Ask an adult to time you.
You need pencil and paper. Write only the answers.

1 9×3.
2 $85 - 26$.
3 One quarter of 48.
4 406×2.
5 $702 - 7$.
6 Write 9000 mm in metres.
7 $45 \div 9$.
8 $\square - 26 = 57$.
9 How many grams in 0.25 kg?
10 $680 \div 2$.
11 Take 85p from £2.20.
12 Halve 138.
13 $15 \times 12 = 180$. What is 15×6?
14 Multiply 420 by 10.

Show most

9

Two, three or four people can play.
Players need pencil and paper to keep their score.
You need a pack of playing cards.
Use the ace to 9 of each suit.

Shuffle the pack.
Deal each person 9 cards.

Round 1   Each player chooses two cards from their hand.
Put them face up on the table side by side.
The player with the biggest two-digit number wins 2 points.
Turn the two cards over.

Round 2   Each player puts down three more cards side by side.
The player with the biggest three-digit number gets 3 points.
Turn the three cards over.

Round 3   Each player puts their last four cards down side by side.
The player with the biggest four-digit number gets 4 points.

If two players both make the biggest number in any round, no points are scored in that round.

The winner is the first to get 30 points.

Change the rules
The player making the smallest number wins the points.

Understand place value
Work out a strategy

10 Rounded

Play with a partner.

You need pencil and paper between you.

Draw this grid.

20	100	50	110	30
80	70	90	60	130
40	120	10	130	40
100	60	110	70	90
30	80	50	120	20

Take turns to choose two of these numbers and add them up.

Round the sum to the nearest 10.

Mark it on the grid with your initial.

Each number on the grid can be marked only once.

The winner is the first to get four of their initials in a straight line.

The line can be horizontal, vertical or diagonal.

Play several times.

Round the sum of two numbers to the nearest 10
Work out a strategy

11 Pick 100

Do this on your own.
You need pencil and paper.

Pick three of these numbers.
They can be the same or different.
The three numbers must total 100.

There are 13 different ways to do it.
How many of them can you find?

Add three two-digit numbers to make a total of 100
Work systematically

12

Ask an adult to read these to you.
You need pencil and paper. Write only the answers.

1   9 multiplied by 4.
2   350 plus 60.
3   Take 10 from 13 plus 14.
4   Halve 186.
5   307 times 2.
6   Write 0.3 as a fraction.
7   Six fives.
8   How many millimetres in 4 centimetres?
9   246 divided by 2.
10 One fifth of 45.
11 What is 3 squared?
12 How many 2p coins make £10?
13 How many sixes in 54?
14 Take 5 grams from 1 kilogram.

13

Ask an adult to time you.
You need pencil and paper. Write only the answers.

1. $5 \times \square = 200$.
2. $160 \div 8$.
3. $63 + 58$.
4. Write **50 129** in words.
5. $\square + 68 = 92$.
6. Five sevens.
7. ⅕ of 100.
8. What is next: 32, 40, 48, … ?
9. Write 6.5 kg in grams.
10. Divide 10 into 690.
11. How many months in 10 years?
12. Approximately, what is 486 – 297?
13. Take £17.81 from £20.
14. Write 0.39 as a fraction.

14

You need pencil and paper. Write only the answers.

1. Does your teapot hold 1 litre, 10 litres or 50 litres?
2. Round 362 to the nearest 10.
3. 6 added to a number makes 21. What is the number?
4. Write 200 millimetres in centimetres.
5. What number is half way between 60 and 90?
6. What must you take from 23 to leave 16?
7. How many minutes in three quarters of an hour?
8. What is the cost of 9 tickets at £3 each?
9. Approximately, what is 58 + 19?
10. What is the change from £1 for 2 lollipops at 29p each?

15

Nines

Two, three or four people can play.
You need two dice.
Each player needs pencil and paper.

Each player should draw a grid like this.

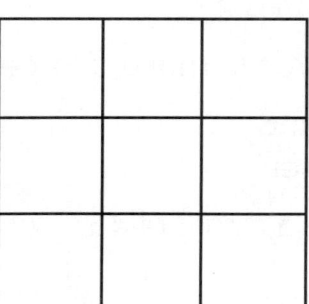

Take turns to roll the dice. Each spot is worth 9.
Write your score on your grid.
Carry on until your grid is full of numbers.

Now take turns to roll the dice again.
If your score is the same as a number on the grid, cross it out.
Otherwise wait for your next turn.

The first to cross out all their numbers wins.

Change the rules
a.   Make each spot worth 7.
b.   Make each spot worth 8.

Practise times-tables (7, 8, 9)

16

Subtract

Two, three or four people can play.

You need a pack of playing cards.

Use the ace to 9 of each suit.

You need pencil and paper to keep the score.

Take turns to be the dealer.

The dealer turns over two cards to make a target.

The first is the tens number and the second is the units number.

With 4 and 5, say, you make a target of 45.

Now deal each player four cards.

Each player arranges their four cards to make a subtraction.

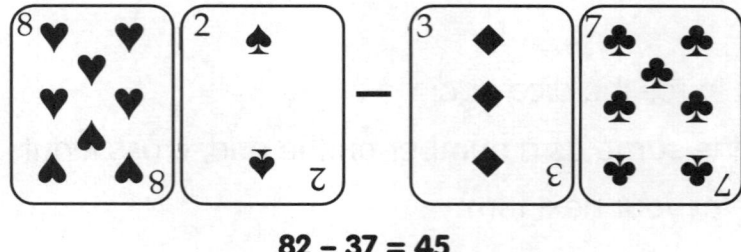

82 − 37 = 45

The answer should be as close to the target as possible.

The player who is closest to the target scores a point.

If two players are equally close they each score a point.

The winner is the player who has the most points after 10 rounds.

Subtract a pair of two-digit numbers
Understand place value

17

Ask an adult to read you these.
You need pencil and paper. Write only the answers.

1. 63 divided by 9.
2. 4 less than 9 times 4.
3. 420 minus 70.
4. 203 times 4.
5. Halve 1000.
6. Square 7.
7. Divide 5700 by 10.
8. Take 45 minutes from 1 hour.
9. Approximately, what is 148 + 98?
10. Five nines.
11. How many metres in 5 kilometres?
12. Find the sum of 6, 18 and 7.
13. Take £41.35 from £50.
14. Take one half from three quarters.

18

Consecutive sums

Two, three or four people can play.
You need pencil and paper between you.

$$11 + 12 + 13 + 14 = 50$$

The first player chooses a starting number from 10 to 30.
The next player adds the number that follows and says the new total.
For example, if you start at 28, take turns to add on 29, 30, 31, 32 …
The player who first reaches a multiple of 10 scores a point.

Take turns to go first.
Each starting number chosen must be different, so keep a record.

The winner is the first player to get 5 points.

Add several two-digit numbers
Recognise multiples of 10

19 Multiply

Do this on your own.

You need pencil and paper.

Choose three different numbers from this set.

Multiply them.
You can get 10 different answers.
Try to list them all.

Change the rules
Three of the numbers must be the same.
What are the answers now?

Multiply three numbers up to 10
Work systematically

20

Ask an adult to time you.

You need pencil and paper. Write only the answers.

1. $408 \div 4$.
2. $8000 - 2991$.
3. Write 1350 cm in metres.
4. $281 - 29$.
5. Half of 57.
6. $72 \div 8$.
7. $65 - \square = 38$.
8. What is missing: 101, $\square$, 95, 92?
9. Approximately, what is $205 \div 49$?
10. Divide 2900 by 100.
11. What is the square of 6?
12. $6 \times \square = 300$.
13. How many centimetres in 2.5 m?
14. Write $^{63}/_{100}$ as a decimal.

21 Max and min

Two, three or four people can play.

You need pencil and paper for each player and a pack of playing cards.

Use the ace to 9 of each suit.

Put the cards face down in a pile.

Each player should draw this on their paper.

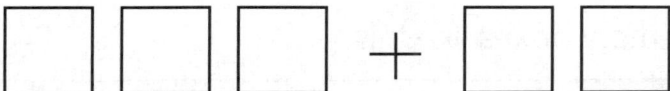

Turn over a card.

Everyone writes that number in one of their boxes.

No changes are allowed after that number is written.

Do this four more times.

The player who makes the biggest answer wins.

Play several times.

Change the rules

a. This time try to make the smallest answer.

☐☐☐ + ☐☐

b. Make the biggest or smallest answer using this.

☐☐☐ − ☐☐

Add or subtract a two-digit number to/from a three-digit number
Understand place value and work out a strategy

22 Spy story

Do this by yourself.
You need pencil and paper.

Spies write messages in code.
They use numbers to stand for letters.
1 is A, 2 is B, and so on.
You will need to work out the rest.

Draw a set of empty boxes like this.

Do these sums in your head. Write the answers in your boxes.

(40 − 13) ÷ 9	90 ÷ 6	1007 − 996	75 ÷ 15
117 − 97	450 ÷ 30		
53 + 86 − 119	1600 ÷ 200	(7 × 9) − 58	
72 ÷ (3 + 9)	(24 × 3) ÷ 72	(400 ÷ 50) + 1	42 − 91 + 67

Now work out the spy's message!

Practise addition, subtraction, multiplication and division

23

You need pencil and paper. Write only the answers.

1. To hire a car costs £25 a day. What does it cost for a week?
2. What is the area of a 9cm by 8cm rectangle?
3. What number is half way between 65 and 125?
4. How many 50p coins in £16.50?
5. It is 2:45 p.m. What time will it be in three quarters of an hour?
6. By how much is 65 miles short of 200 miles?
7. How many children had 9 sweets each from a bag of 108?
8. How many minutes in 4 hours?
9. Round 827 to the nearest 10.
10. 2 apples cost the same as 3 pears. Which is cheaper: an apple or a pear?

24

Ask an adult to read you these.
You need pencil and paper. Write only the answers.

1. 305 times 3.
2. Is 37 a prime number?
3. Nine sixes.
4. Half of 95.
5. One quarter of 800.
6. Write 1.9 as a mixed number.
7. How many eights in 24?
8. Write 18000 metres in kilometres.
9. Take 9 from 3 times 5.
10. Write two and a half as a decimal.
11. What fraction of £1 is 25p?
12. Take 27 minutes from 1 hour.
13. What is half way between 97 and 31?
14. How many 5p coins make £20?

25

Ask an adult to time you.
You need pencil and paper. Write only the answers.

1. Double 87.
2. 36 divided by 10.
3. 84 + 97.
4. Divide 7 into 28.
5. Write 0.8 as a fraction.
6. Write **61 039** in words.
7. 36 + ☐ = 62.
8. Find the product of 6 and 7.
9. Write 4.25 litres in millilitres.
10. $\frac{1}{100}$ of 1 metre.
11. What is next: 27, 36, 45, … ?
12. 630 ÷ 6.
13. 4 × ☐ = 800.
14. Write $\frac{7}{10}$ as a decimal

26

Number chains

Two or three people can play.

You need some dried beans (or buttons) and pencil and paper for the last part.

The first player chooses a three-digit number, such as 367.

Take turns to follow these rules.

If the number is odd, add 3 and take a bean.

if the number is even, halve it.

Keep going. Stop when you get to 1.

The winner is the player with the most beans.

Play several times. Choose a different starting number each time.

Make a record of the longest chain you can make.

Recognise odd and even numbers
Halve two- and three-digit numbers

Three numbers

27

Two or three people can play.

Another person who has a watch with a second hand acts as a timekeeper.

You each need pencil and paper.

You need three dice between you.

Each player should write a list of the numbers 1 to 30.

The timekeeper rolls the three dice and starts timing one minute.

Everyone tries to make a number on their list.

For each number, use each of the three numbers rolled once.

Use any operations $(+, -, \times$ or $\div)$.

For example, with 3, 5 and 4 you could make: 17   because $17 = 4 \times 5 - 3$

or: 38   because $38 = 43 - 5$ …

Write your calculation next to the number.

Keep going – try to make more numbers on the list.

After one minute, the timekeeper says 'Stop' and rolls the dice again.

Now use the new numbers rolled.

The winner is the first player to make all the numbers.

Change the rules

Make the numbers 31 to 50.

Use knowledge of number facts and times-tables
Think flexibly and eliminate what won't work

28 Higgledy piggledy

Start this on your own.

You need paper, a pencil and some scissors.

Make 9 number cards.

Arrange your cards in the shapes of the letters.

Make each straight line of 3 numbers add up to the same total.

a.   Use the cards 1 to 7.
     Make each line of H add to 13.

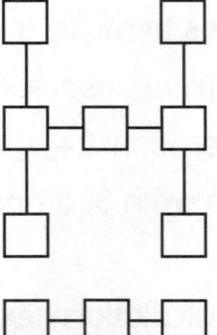

b.   Use the cards 1 to 9.
     Make each line of E add to 15.

c.   Use the cards 1 to 7.
     Make each line of N add to 12.

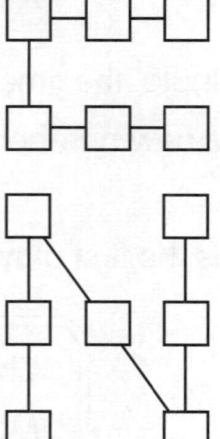

Record how you did each one.

Now ask your family to try.

Add several small numbers
Think logically to eliminate what won't work

29

Ask an adult to read you these.
You need pencil and paper. Write only the answers.

1. Double 77.
2. 10 squared.
3. Write 7.25 as a mixed number.
4. Double three quarters.
5. One tenth of £2.
6. Divide 366 by 6.
7. Seven nines.
8. Write 315 millimetres in centimetres.
9. Take 11 from half of 26.
10. How many sevens in 56?
11. Take 36 minutes from 1 hour.
12. Is 56 a prime number?
13. How many fours in 32?
14. What fraction of £1 is 10p?

30

Remainders

Two, three or four people can play.

You need pencil and paper to keep the score, a dice and a pack of cards.

Use the ace to 9 of each suit.

Shuffle the cards. Put them face down in a pile.
Take turns. Roll the two dice and find the total.
Draw two cards and make a two-digit number.
With, say, 7 and 9 you can make 79 or 97.
Divide your two-digit number by your dice total.
The remainder is your score for that round.
Watch out – it might be zero!

The winner is the first to get a total score of 80.

Divide two-digit numbers by a number from 2 to 12
Find and add up the remainders.

31

You need pencil and paper. Write only the answers.

1. Double a number is 56. What is the number?
2. Is the sum of 120 and 91 odd or even?
3. Does a full kitchen bucket hold about 1 litre, 10 litres or 100 litres?
4. Gita walked one quarter of 1 kilometre. How many metres is that?
5. It is 9:25 a.m. What time was it an hour and a half ago?
6. Round 827 to the nearest 100.
7. Trainers cost £35.65. What change do you get from £40?
8. The side of a square lawn is 12.5 metres. How long is its perimeter?
9. Tickets are £9 each. How many can you get for £75?
10. What temperature is shown on this thermometer?

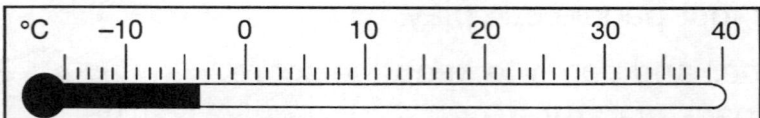

32

Ask an adult to time you.
You need pencil and paper. Write only the answers.

1. Three-quarters of 36.
2. 9×8.
3. Write 35 km in metres.
4. Halve 132.
5. $82 - 57$.
6. $48 \div 6$.
7. $\square - 42 = 29$.
8. What is missing: 62, $\square$, 52, 47 ?
9. Take 7 millilitres from 2 litres.
10. Round 4526 to the nearest 1000.
11. $1/100$ of 2 metres.
12. $3 \times \square = 600$.
13. Write 0.77 as a fraction.
14. 63×5.

33 Connect four

Play with a partner.

You need pencil and paper between you and a pack of playing cards.

Use the ace to 9 of each suit.

Draw this on the paper.

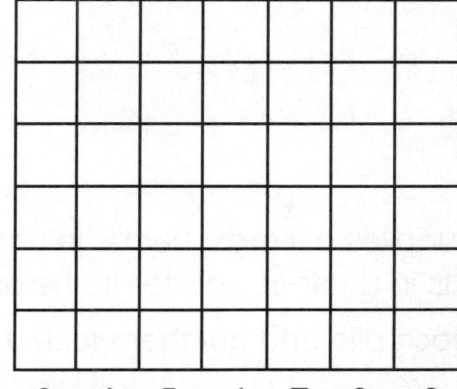

Multiples of: 3 4 5 6 7 8 9

Put the cards face down in a pile.

Take turns to turn over two cards.

If you draw 4 and 8, say, you can make 84 or 48.

Try to make a multiple of 3, 4, 5, 6, 7, 8 or 9.

Say what your number is a multiple of.

For example, with 48 you could say '48 is a multiple of 6'.

Write your initial in an empty space in the correct column.

Start with the space at the bottom of each column and work up.

If you can't do it, or if the column is full, your turn ends.

The winner is the first to get four of their initials in a line in any direction.

Recognise multiples of 3 to 9
Work out a strategy

34 Tables race

Play with a partner who has a watch with a second hand.

You need a pack of playing cards.

Use the ace to 10 of each suit.

Make four piles of cards: hearts in one, clubs in another, diamonds in another, spades in the another.

Shuffle each pile and put them face down.

Start when your partner says 'Go'.

Turn over the top card of the first pile.

Say 6 times the number.

If your partner says you are right, keep the card.

If not, put the card back at the bottom of the pile.

Carry on until you have won all that pile.

Now start on the second pile. Say 7 times the number.

For the third pile say 8 times the number.

For the last pile say 9 times the number.

When you win the last card say 'Stop'.

How many seconds did you take?

Play again. Can you beat your record?

Practise times-tables (6, 7, 8, 9)

35 Kite puzzle

Do this on your own.

This kite is made up of lots of triangles.
Some of them are inside others.
How many of the triangles can you count?

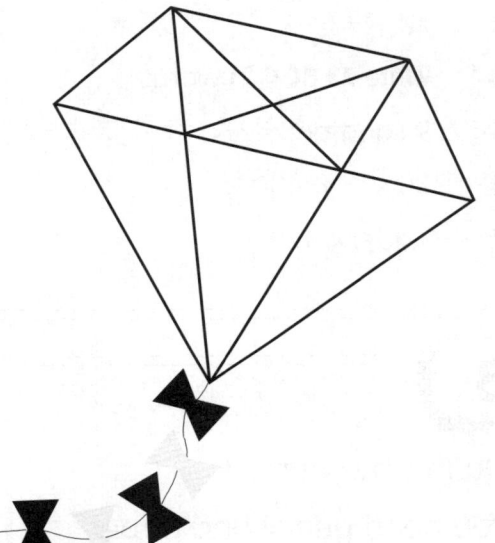

Now ask your family and friends.
Can they find as many of the triangles as you can?

Recognise triangles
Work out a strategy

36

Ask an adult to read you these.
You need pencil and paper. Write only the answers.

1. 40 multiplied by 30.
2. Halve 174.
3. Take 1995 from 4000.
4. One quarter of 600.
5. Add 7 to 15 minus 8.
6. Is 57 a prime number?
7. Half of 1.5.
8. Roughly, what is 701 divided by 11?
9. Write one fifth as a decimal.
10. What fraction of £1 is 20p?
11. Write 460 centimetres in metres.
12. 2¼ take away one half.
13. One tenth of 1 centimetre.
14. What is 0.3 plus 0.2?

37

Ask an adult to time you.
You need pencil and paper. Write only the answers.

1. 52 multiplied by 8.
2. Write $^{23}/_{100}$ as a decimal.
3. 72 ÷ 9.
4. Write **73 804** in words.
5. 9 squared.
6. 50 × ☐ = 400.
7. Add 0.4 to 0.7.
8. $^{1}/_{10}$ of 3cm.
9. ☐ + 65 = 91.
10. One sixth of 300.
11. How many millilitres is 3.75 litres?
12. 803 − 789.
13. 17 × 3 = 51. What is 17 × 6?
14. 820 ÷ 4.

38

Magic multiples

Do this by yourself.
You need pencil and paper.

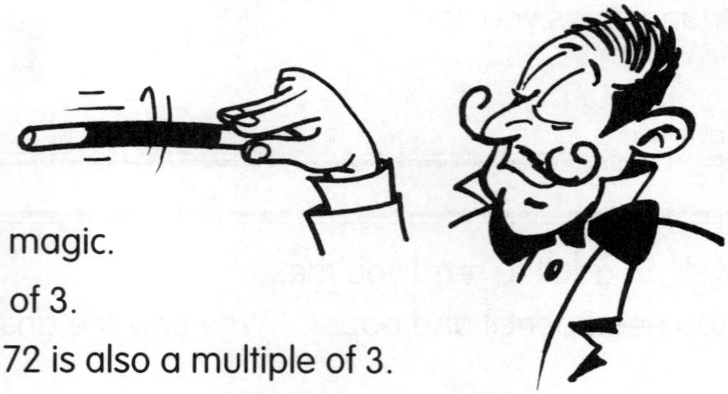

Some two-digit multiples are magic.
For example, 27 is a multiple of 3.
When you reverse the digits, 72 is also a multiple of 3.

List all the multiples of 6 between 10 and 100.
How many of them are still multiples of 6 when you reverse the digits?

Now try multiples of 9 between 10 and 100.
Then try some three-digit multiples of 9.
What did you discover?

Recognise multiples of 6 and 9

Space travel

Play this with a partner.

F(1) L(2) Y(3) I(4) N(5) G(6)   S(7) A(8) U(9) C(10) E(11) R(12)

Each letter has a value.

Multiply the numbers in the words below.

Your partner should check and say if you are right.

1	IS	5	AS	9	LIE
2	AN	6	FLY	10	INN
3	IF	7	ILL	11	NAG
4	US	8	FUN	12	CALL

Think of more words using the letters of FLYING SAUCER.

Ask your partner to work out what they are worth.

You must say if your partner is right.

Find the product of two or more numbers
Use times-tables facts

40 Lay them out

Three or four people can play.
You need a pack of playing cards.
Use cards 2 to 10 of each suit.

Shuffle the 36 cards.
Lay them out face up in a 6 by 6 square.

Take turns.
Secretly choose two cards that are next to each other.
Without saying what they are call out their product.
The other players try to find them, or another pair of neighbouring cards with the same product.

The product of 7 and 5 is 35
$7 \times 5 = 35$

The first player to call out a correct pair of cards wins them.
If the cards get too far apart, push them in to close the gaps.

Carry on until all the cards have been won.
The player who wins the most pairs wins the game.

Recognise multiples and factors
Practise times-tables

Ask an adult to read you these.
You need pencil and paper. Write only the answers.

1. Twelve threes plus two.
2. How many sixes in 42?
3. Three tenths of 1 metre.
4. Add 48 to 88.
5. Eight squared.
6. One fifth of 60.
7. Divide 20 into 1000.
8. How many millimetres in 7 metres?
9. What is 1.8 plus 0.3?
10. Divide 640 by 8.
11. Multiply 0.8 by 5.
12. Add 8 to 26 minus 11.
13. How many hours in 3 days?
14. Write three fifths as a decimal.

42

You need pencil and paper. Write only the answers.

1. Write **fifty thousand, five hundred and five** in figures.
2. The temperature drops by 20°C from 13°C. What is it now?
3. James cut 33 cm from 2 metres of tape. How much is left?
4. What is the remainder when 653 is divided by 10?
5. What is the area of a field which is 100 m long by 50 m wide?
6. A jug holds 1.5 litres. What do 9 jugs hold?
7. How long is it from 9:20 p.m. to midnight?
8. How many millilitres is one quarter of a litre?
9. Round 487 to the nearest hundred.
10. A box holds 12 eggs. How many boxes are needed to hold 100 eggs?

43

Take a square

Two, three or four people can play.
You need some beans.

Take turns to go first.
The first player chooses a starting number from 10 to 200.
In turn, subtract any square number (1, 4, 9, 16, 25, 36, 49, 64, 81 …)
You must not go past zero.
The player who reaches zero **exactly** gets a bean.

Play lots of times. The winner is the one to get most beans.

For this part you need pencil and paper.
Work out the least number of turns for each number from 30 to 50.

Recognise square numbers and practise subtraction
Work out a strategy

44

Ask an adult to time you.
You need pencil and paper. Write only the answers.

1. $\frac{1}{100}$ of £7.
2. 94 – 56.
3. 320 ÷ 8.
4. $\frac{1}{10}$ of 5 metres.
5. 6001 – 4989.
6. ☐ + 4 + 9 = 21.
7. 630 ÷ 70.
8. Write 8.5 metres in millimetres.
9. Write a prime number between 10 and 20.
10. Round 6327 to the nearest 100.
11. Write **40 205** in words.
12. 86 × 7 = 602. What is 86 × 14?
13. What fraction of 1 cm is 2 mm?
14. Find the product of 25 and 5.

45 On the farm

Do this by yourself.
You need pencil and paper.

The names of 10 animals are hidden in this puzzle.
Move up, down or sideways to find them, but not diagonally.

A	C	H	A	T	L	L
T	N	E	R	B	U	F
L	A	M	F	L	A	O
O	C	B	T	D	C	A
W	G	O	A	O	G	L

Each letter has a value. A is 1, B is 2, C is 3, and so on.
You will need to work out the rest.
Add up the numbers in the animals' names.
Which animals have these totals?

- **a.** 22
- **b.** 24
- **c.** 26
- **d.** 28
- **e.** 27
- **f.** 34
- **g.** 39
- **h.** 41
- **i.** 43
- **j.** 47

Add several one- and two-digit numbers

46 Fifteens

Two, three or four people can play.
You need two dice.
Each player needs pencil and paper.

Each player should draw a grid like this.

Take turns to roll the dice. Each spot is worth 15.
Write your score on your grid.
Carry on until your grid is full of numbers.

Now take turns to roll the dice again.
If your score is the same as a number on the grid, cross it out.
Otherwise wait for your next turn.

The first to cross out all their numbers wins.

> **Change the rules**
> Make each spot worth 20 or 25.
> For a challenge, try 16.

Multiply by 15, 20, 25 or 16

47

Ask an adult to read you these.
You need pencil and paper. Write only the answers.

1. Divide 250 by 50.
2. Take £14.38 from £20.
3. 10 times 10 times 10.
4. Is 45 a multiple of 4?
5. Eight sevens.
6. Double 236.
7. Write 50 per cent as a fraction.
8. 32 × 26 = 832. What is 32 × 13?
9. How many 18p pens can I get for £1?
10. Add 500 grams to 1 kilogram.
11. Decrease 72 by 49.
12. Approximately, what is 11 times 51?
13. Add 9 to one third of 24.
14. 7 multiplied by 18.

48

You need pencil and paper. Write only the answers.

1. How much are 10 books at £3.75 each?
2. How many 40 cm ribbons can you cut from 6 metres?
3. Write in figures **one hundred thousand and sixty**.
4. How long is it from 7:25 p.m. to 9:15 p.m?
5. Round £90.99 to the nearest pound.
6. The perimeter of a square is 10 cm. How long is one side?
7. What is the difference between £5.67 and £6.28?
8. A number multiplied by itself is 64. What is the number?
9. What must I add to 86 to make 132?
10. How many small cubes in this cuboid?

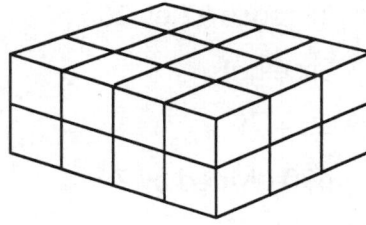

49 Sort it out

Do this by yourself.

You need pencil and paper.

Copy and complete this diagram.

Numbers from 40 to 100

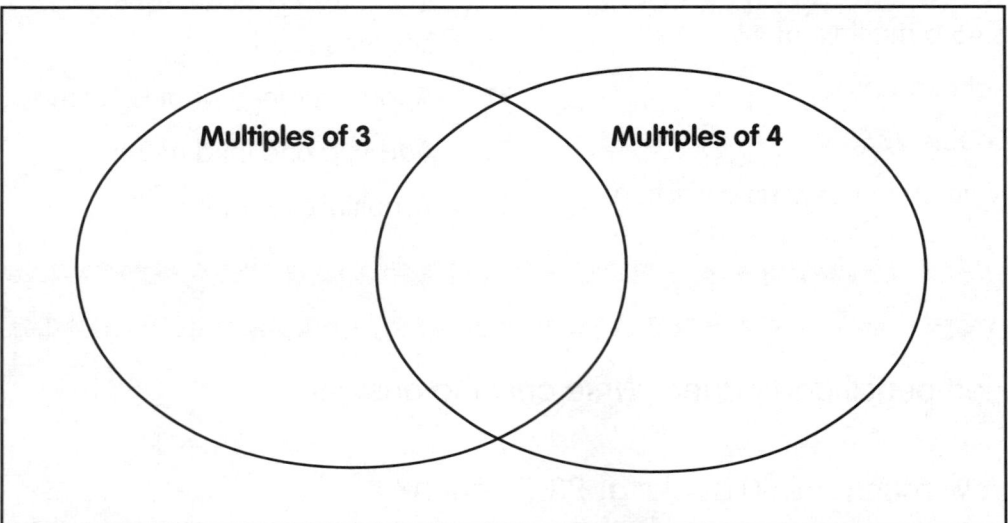

Recognise multiples of 3, 4 and 12
Use a two-way Venn diagram

50

Ask an adult to time you.
You need pencil and paper. Write only the answers.

1. $7 + \square + 6 = 25$
2. Double 138.
3. $3007 - 1992$.
4. Increase 27 by 35.
5. Six eights.
6. $52 + 79$.
7. 490 divided by 7.
8. Roughly, what is 59×59?
9. $\square + 68 = 123$
10. 24×6.
11. $\frac{1}{100}$ of £12.
12. What number multiplied by itself is 81?
13. $135 - 82$.
14. How many grams is 6.25 kg?

51 Make 200

Two, three or four people can play.

You need pencil and paper for each player and a pack of playing cards.

Use the ace to 9 of each suit.

Put the cards face down in a pile.

Each player should draw this on their paper.

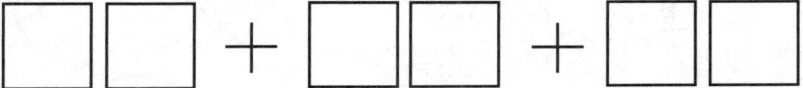

Turn over one card.

Everyone writes that number in one of their boxes.

No changes are allowed after that number is written.

Do this five more times.

The player whose sum is closest to 200 scores a point.

The winner is the first player to get 10 points.

Change the rules

Deal six cards all at once.

The winner is then the player whose sum is closest to 200 after 2 minutes.

Add three two-digit numbers
Understand place value and work out a strategy

52 Bugs

Two or three people can play.

You need two dice and pencil and paper between you.

Draw these bugs on the paper.

Bugs with numbers: 56, 72, 39, 110, 60, 120, 35, 64, 28, 144, 63, 42, 99, 48, 55, 90

Take turns to roll the two dice.

Find the total of your two numbers.

If you can, you must cross out a bug.

The bug you choose must have your total as a factor.

If there is no bug to cross out, score 25.

When all the bugs are crossed out, who has the lowest score?
That player is the winner.

Change the rules

Play with just one dice.

Recognise multiples of 2 to 12

53 Next birthday

Do this by yourself.
You need pencil and paper.

1. How many weeks to your next birthday?
   How many hours to your next birthday?

2. How long do you spend in bed each week?
   How long will you spend in bed before your birthday?

3. How many hours of TV do you watch each week?
   How many hours of TV will you watch before your birthday?

4. How much pocket money do you get each week?
   How much pocket money will you get before your birthday?

Practise long multiplication

54

Ask an adult to read these to you.
You need pencil and paper. Write only the answers.

1. Three nines.
2. Three tenths of 50p.
3. Take 500 millilitres from 2 litres.
4. Share 60 equally among 4.
5. Is 42 a multiple of 3?
6. 9 times 17.
7. One hundredth of 8 metres.
8. One quarter of 1000.
9. How many metres is 1.3 kilometres?
10. Write 10 per cent as a fraction.
11. How many seconds in 5 minutes?
12. 38 plus one third of 15.
13. Approximately, what is 399 ÷ 9?
14. Halve 658.

55

Ask an adult to time you.
You need pencil and paper. Write only the answers.

1. 15 times 7.
2. Halve 476.
3. 81 ÷ 9.
4. Write **90 340** in words.
5. 126 − 55.
6. 34 × 5.
7. 32 + 6 = 40 − ☐.
8. Round 5109 to the nearest 10.
9. Take £1.17 from £10.
10. ☐ × 5 = 525.
11. What is next: 70, 63, 56, … ?
12. $\frac{1}{10}$ of £7.
13. 18 ÷ 4.
14. Approximately, what is 139 ÷ 19?

56

You need pencil and paper. Write only the answers.

1. What is the cost of 9 bags of potatoes at 45p a bag?
2. Write in order, largest first: $\frac{3}{10}$, $\frac{2}{5}$, $\frac{1}{4}$, $\frac{7}{20}$.
3. Round 48.6 to the nearest whole number.
4. The perimeter of a square is 200 millimetres. What is its area?
5. How many cakes at 35p each can you buy for £5?
6. What must you multiply 25 by to get 200?
7. What is the remainder when 62 is divided by 9?
8. How long is it from 10:15 a.m. to midnight?
9. Write a prime number between 30 and 40.
10. What will the day and date be after 20 days?

Tuesday
March
20

57 Burgers

Play this with a partner.

You each need a dice and pencil and paper.

Someone says 'Go'.

Both roll your dice.

Work out the cost of that number of burgers at £1.35 each.

Write your change from £10 on your paper.

Do this five times each.

Now add up your five lots of change.

When you have both finished, work out your scores.

Scoring

The player who first finished adding the change scores a point.

The player with the greatest amount of change also scores a point.

Play several times. The winner is the first to get 10 points.

Change the rules

Alter the price of the burgers.

Find the change from £20.

Multiply pounds and pence by 1, 2, 3, 4, 5 or 6
Work out change from £10; find a total amount of money

58
Can you cube it?

Two, three or four people can play.

You need a pack of playing cards and pencil and paper to keep the score.

Use the ace to 9 of each suit.

Shuffle the cards.

Deal everyone 2 cards face up.

Each player makes a two-digit number.

With, say, 2 and 3 you could make 23 or 32.

> A prime number scores 2.
> A square number scores 3.
> A cube number scores 5.

23 is prime

Return the cards to the pack and shuffle again.

Keep going.

The winner is the first to get a total score of 50.

Change the rules

Deal 3 cards each and make three-digit numbers.

A multiple of 3 scores 3.

A multiple of 5 scores 5.

A multiple of 7 scores 7.

Recognise square, cube and prime numbers
Practise short division and recognise multiples of 3, 5 or 7

59

Ask an adult to read you these.
You need pencil and paper. Write only the answers.

1. 6.3 divided by 9.
2. Divide 490 by 70.
3. Increase £123 by £18.
4. 10 per cent of £1.90.
5. 25 multiplied by 6.
6. Half of 155.
7. Six nines.
8. What fraction of £1 is 1p?
9. Write 50 per cent as a decimal.
10. Take £6.43 from £10.
11. Add 15 to half of 36.
12. Approximately, what is 162 − 88?
13. One sixth of 24 miles.
14. 19 multiplied by 7.

60 One thousand

Play with a partner.
Each player needs pencil and paper.

84 × 12 is 1008

Take turns to go first.

The first player chooses a starting number between 1 and 250.

Each of you then says what **whole number** you will multiply the starting number by to get as close as possible to 1000.

You can be under 1000 or over 1000.

Now each do your multiplication and record your answer.

Work out how far you are from 1000.

The player who is closest to 1000 scores a point.

The first to get 10 points wins the game.

Estimate how many times 1000 divides by a chosen number
Practise short or long multiplication

61

Ask an adult to time you.
You need pencil and paper. Write only the answers..

1. ☐ − 64 = 76.
2. 6012 − 2996.
3. 73 + 88.
4. 78 − 5 = ☐ + 3.
5. 1% of £23.
6. 56 ÷ 7.
7. 9 times 0.4.
8. How many days in 15 weeks?
9. Approximately, what is 78 × 18.
10. ☐ + 7 + 8 = 43
11. 45 × 6.
12. What is next: 3770, 3870, 3970, … ?
13. Write 20.5 litres in millilitres.
14. 15 × 48 = 720. What is 15 × 24?

62 Make 100

Start this on your own.
You need a pencil, paper and some scissors.
Make 7 number cards.

[1] [2] [3] [4] [5] [6] [7]

Arrange your cards to make a total of 100.
Use each card once and only once.

For example, [5] [2] + [1] [3] + [4] [6] + [7] = 118

Can you do better than this?
Ask others to try.
Find different ways of doing it.

Find a total of one- and two-digit numbers
Think logically to eliminate what won't work

63 Lions

Ask all your family to join in.

```
L  I  O  N   T  A  M  E  R
3  4  5  6   10 11 12 13 14
```

Add up the numbers standing for the letters.
Find words that are worth these.

Two-letter words

1	11	4	17
2	21	5	14
3	23	6	15

Three letter words

7	12	10	35
8	24	11	28
9	10	12	34

Secretly make another word using the letters of LION TAMER.
Work out what it is worth and tell everyone.
Can they guess what your word is?

Add several small numbers

64 Target

Do this by yourself.

You need pencil and paper.

Each time, use three different numbers from this set.

(76) (42) (69) (54) (85)

Copy and complete these.

1. ... + ... + ... = **181**
2. ... + ... + ... = **203**
3. ... + ... + ... = **230**
4. ... + ... + ... = **208**
5. ... + ... + ... = **187**
6. ... + ... + ... = **165**

Add three two-digit numbers
Work out a strategy

65

Ask an adult to read you these.
You need pencil and paper. Write only the answers.

1. Three quarters of 1000.
2. Eight nines.
3. 7 times 25.
4. Seven tenths of 100.
5. 20 per cent of £20.
6. Take 11 from 9 plus 8.
7. Decrease £115 by £26.
8. Take £39.26 from £50.
9. 5 millimetres less than 30 centimetres.
10. What fraction of £2 is 50p?
11. Add 70 centimetres to half a metre.
12. Share 408 equally among 8.
13. What is the next prime number after 47?
14. Take 991 from 1006.

66

Drinks

Any number of people can play.
Each player needs pencil and paper.

Each letter stands for a number.

A	B	C	D	E	F	G	H	I	J	K	L	M
1	2	3	4	5	6	7	8	9	10	11	12	13

N	O	P	Q	R	S	T	U	V	W	X	Y	Z
14	15	16	17	18	19	20	21	22	23	24	25	26

The first player says: "Choose a drink".
Take turns to choose a different drink and write it on your paper.
Under each letter write its number.
Multiply your largest number by your smallest number.
The player with the greatest answer scores 3 points.

On the next round, choose something different.
It could be a colour, a footballer, a town, an author, a flower …
The winner is the first player to get 30 points.

Change the rules

a. Add up all your numbers.
   The greatest (or least) total wins.

b. Divide your largest number by the smallest.
   The smallest (or largest) answer wins.

Practise short and long multiplication
Work out a strategy

67

You need pencil and paper. Write only the answers.

1. How heavy are 6 bags of hay each weighing 19 kg?
2. 8 km is about 5 miles. About how many kilometres is 30 miles?
3. 78 added to a number makes 132. What is the number?
4. It is 2.15 p.m. What time was it three and a half hour ago?
5. Anil saved 5p on each day in May. How much did he save?
6. Round 89.2 to the nearest whole number.
7. Put in order, smallest first: 1.23, 2.3, 0.33, 2.13.
8. Approximately, what is 289 + 48?
9. Write all the prime numbers between 60 and 70.
10. Does an egg-cup hold 5 ml, 50 ml or 500 ml?

68

Ask an adult to time you.
You need pencil and paper. Write only the answers.

1. 32 − ☐ = 17 + 8.
2. 50% of £34.
3. 29 times 5.
4. ☐ ÷ 6 = 51.
5. 131 − 89.
6. 42 ÷ 7.
7. ³⁄₈ of 16.
8. Write **80 042** in words.
9. Roughly, what is 587 ÷ 29?
10. 6 books at £3.49 each cost …?
11. Find the product of 16 and 8.
12. How much altogether is £14.73 and £28.42?
13. What is missing: 87, 78, ☐, 60?
14. Write all the factors of 15.

Square puzzles

Do this by yourself.

You need pencil and paper and 24 matches or cocktail sticks.

1 Arrange 17 matches to make 6 equal squares like this.

Now take away 5 matches, leaving 3 equal squares.

Sketch what you did.

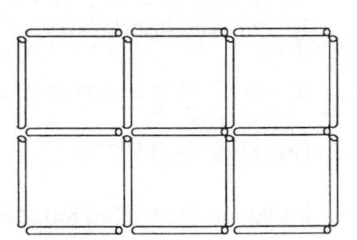

2 Arrange 16 matches to make 5 equal squares like this.

Remove 3 matches, then replace them to make 4 equal squares.

Sketch what you did.

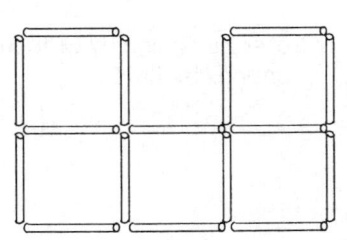

3 Arrange 20 matches to make 7 equal squares like this.

Remove 3 matches, then replace them to make 5 equal squares.

Sketch what you did.

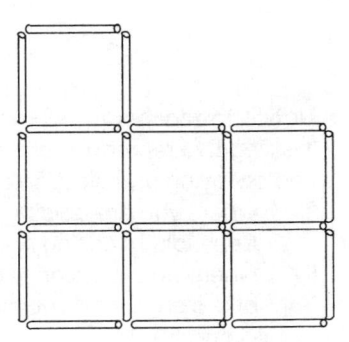

Now ask your family to try.

Recognise different shapes made of squares
Think logically and visualise rearrangements

PUBLISHED BY THE PRESS SYNDICATE OF THE UNIVERSITY OF CAMBRIDGE
The Pitt Building, Trumpington Street, Cambridge CB2 1RP, United Kingdom

CAMBRIDGE UNIVERSITY PRESS
The Edinburgh Building, Cambridge CB2 2RU, United Kingdom
40 West 20th Street, New York, NY 10011-4211, USA
10 Stamford Road, Oakleigh, Melbourne 3166, Australia

© Cambridge University Press 1998

First published 1998

Printed in the United Kingdom at the University Press, Cambridge

A catalogue record for this book is available from the British Library

ISBN 0 521 64924 2 paperback

Cover illustration by Graham Round
Cartoons by Tim Sell

Notice to teachers
It is illegal to reproduce any part of this work in material form (including photocopying and electronic storage) except in the following circumstances:
(i) where you are abiding by a licence granted to your school by the Copyright Licensing Agency;
(ii) where no such licence exists, or where you wish to exceed the terms of a licence, and you have gained the written permission of Cambridge University Press;
(iii) where you are allowed to reproduce without permission under the provisions of Chapter 3 of the Copyright, Designs and Patents Act 1988.